A Very Very Very Dark Matter

MARTIN McDONAGH

A Very Very Very Dark Matter

ff

FABER & FABER

First published in 2018
by Faber and Faber Limited
The Bindery, 51 Hatton Garden
London EC1N 8HN

Revised December 2018

Typeset by Country Setting, Kingsdown, Kent CT14 8ES
Printed in England by CPI Group (UK) Ltd, Croydon CR0 4YY

© Martin McDonagh, 2018

Martin McDonagh is hereby identified as author
of this work in accordance with Section 77 of
the Copyright, Designs and Patents Act 1988

A CIP record for this book is available from the British Library

ISBN 978-0-571-34691-2

Printed and bound in the UK on FSC® certified paper in line with our continuing
commitment to ethical business practices, sustainability and the environment.
For further information see faber.co.uk/environmental-policy

Characters

in order of appearance

Narrator

Marjory

Hans Christian Andersen

Edvard Collin

Ingrid

Press Man

Dirk *and* Barry

Ogechi

Charles Dickens

Catherine

Kate, Walter *and* Charles Jnr

A Very Very Very Dark Matter was first performed at
the Bridge Theatre, London, on 12 October 2018.
The cast, in order of appearance, was as follows:

Narrator Tom Waits
Marjory Johnetta Eula'Mae Ackles
Hans Jim Broadbent
Edvard Lee Knight
Ingrid Audrey Hayhurst / Amelia Walter /
    Annabelle Westenholz-Smith
Press Man Paul Bradley
Dirk Ryan Pope
Barry Graeme Hawley
Ogechi Kundai Kanyama
Dickens Phil Daniels
Catherine Elizabeth Berrington
Kate Audrey Hayhurst / Amelia Walter /
    Annabelle Westenholz-Smith
Walter Regan Garcia / Leo Hart / Austin Taylor
Charles Jnr Alistair Benson / Noah Brignull /
    James Roberts
Crowd Jamie McKie, Alice Selwyn, Anthony Taylor

Other parts played by members of the company

Director Matthew Dunster
Designer Anna Fleischle
Music James Maloney
Lighting Designer Philip Gladwell
Sound Designer George Dennis
Illusions Chris Fisher
Video Designer Finn Ross
Wigs and Prosthetic Designer Susanna Peretz
Fight Directors Rachel Bown-Williams and
    Ruth Cooper-Brown, RC Annie Ltd
Assistant Director Nimmo Ismail
Associate Designer Liam Bunster
Illusions Associate John Bulleid
Video Associate Ash Woodward
Casting Director Amy Ball
US Casting by Telsey & Company / William Cantler, CSA;
    Karyn Casl, CSA; and Adam Caldwell, CSA
Costume Supervisor Ilona Karas
*Props Supervisor*s Marcus Hall Props

A VERY VERY VERY DARK MATTER

Part One

SCENE ONE

An attic in Copenhagen in the late 1800s. Various beautifully crafted but peculiar marionettes hang across the dark wooden walls, or are strewn across the dirty floor; puppets such as tarantulas, crabs, a scarecrow, a woodsman, as well as more ordinary animals such as a kitten, seahorses, pigeons, hummingbirds, etc., all very colourful. There's also a large concertina hanging on the back wall. A high window is in the back wall stage right, with a very poorly made wooden ladder beneath it. Outside the window is a view of the low rooftops and waterways of Copenhagen at dusk.

As the play begins, a three-foot by three-foot mahogany box, suspended by a thick rope from an unseen roof beam, slowly and theatrically swings into view and, like a pendulum, swings back and forth from left to right, but does so as if in slow motion. There is a circular hole near the top of the front of the box, and a thin slot at the bottom of the same side, just enough for a few sheets of paper to be slid into or out of. We do not see the back side of the box as yet, nor properly through the hole or the slot, but from the shifts of the shadows and light, we know that there is something alive and moving inside. The gravel-voiced narrator coughs to clear his throat, then speaks . . .

Narrator You could call it a puzzle, or you could call it a poem. *I* wouldn't call it *either*, really, but you could. I mean, a *person* could, y'know . . .?

The fingers of a small black female hand appear in the circular hole, gently holding on to its edges for a couple of pendulum swings, then the eye of a very small black woman appears behind it.

If you were a Congolese pygmy, imprisoned for sixteen years in a three-foot by three-foot mahogany box, with just some paper and a pencil for company . . . how would you go about hanging yourself?

Some sheaves of parchment, written on in a beautiful hand, are slid out through the slot and gently flutter down to the attic floor.

You've got no rope. You've got no shoelaces. You've only got one foot left in fact. So how would you go about hanging yourself? It's been on your mind for a while now.

As the Narrator continues, the box gently turns and the swinging slows, to reveal that its back wall is made of glass, with a hole and a slot in identical positions to the other side, and, inside the box, striking a match to throw a little light on the subject, is, as we have described, a tiny black woman, elegantly dressed, a small black muslin bag covering her missing left foot.

You're smart. You're one of the most iconic writers of your generation, in fact, aside from your sister. But you're a pygmy, and you're a woman, and you were born in the Congo in 1869, the worst time for anybody to be born anywhere ever, let alone a black dwarf. So no one may know that you even existed, let alone astonished the fifteen generations that are left to come after you. So what are you going to do?

She sits down, and behind her we can make out that the entire interior of the box is covered in the writings and notes and formulae of a tiny hand.

Your husband's dead so he can't help you, and your children are dead so they can't help you. Your sister's got her own troubles, in her own shoelaceless box in nineteenth-century fucking England. So what are you going to do?

She lights a small cigar and sits there, gazing out as she quietly smokes, the match still lit.

But maybe you aren't going to hang yourself at all. Maybe that's being a little too defeatist. Maybe you're going to write your way out of it? (*Pause.*) Yeah, that's it. Maybe you're going to write your way out of it.

She looks at us a moment, then blows the match out, and the lights fade on the box, then on the attic, till only the blue in the dark skies outside the window remain. Fireworks begin to pop in those same distant skies.

SCENE TWO

A fancy open-air Copenagen garden party, following on in time from the last scene. Numerous guests, including Edvard Collin, his eight-year-old daughter Ingrid, a Press Man with the word 'Press' on a card in his hat band, and a few other dignitaries and their well-dressed children, stand and listen to the gangly and peculiarly dressed Hans Christian Andersen, on a raised dais at a lectern, reading out, for the very first time, 'The Little Mermaid', just as those same fireworks start going off in the skies behind.

Hans 'And the little mermaid lifted her glorified eyes heavenward, and felt them, for the first time, filling with tears . . .' Fireworks?! For me?! For Hans Christian Andersen?! (*Pause.*) I said 'Fireworks? For me? For Hans Christian . . .' (*Quietly.*) Say yes . . .

Edvard Yes!

The guests all clap.

Hans Fireworks?! And clapping?! For the lowly Hans Christian Andersen? I might cry! I knew my new story was wonderful and one for the ages but fireworks! Gosh! Invented by Chinamen, fireworks, a little known fact. Fireworks and *walls*, they invented. And who could live without either? No one! That said, as my old mum used to point out, another little known fact, the Chinese? Absolute savages. They eat the puppies that belong to their children and then, if they're still hungry, they eat their children! (*To the Press Man.*) Don't write that down you, you old 'Write-that-downer'! For small normal children might get frightened of that savage image and small normal children are both the lifeblood of Denmark and my core fan base so, y'know? Lovely Edvard Collin? Where was I?

Edvard The little mermaid has refused to kill the prince and now it appears that she may die.

Hans Die? Really? Of course, 'Really'! It's my story, isn't it? (*Reading again.*) 'Glorified eyes heavenward . . . filled with tears . . . ' Ah yes. 'On the ship in which she had left her beautiful prince, she saw him and his beautiful bride searching for her . . .'

Two 'red men' have appeared: naked to the waist, heads and torsos totally covered in what looks like blood, strange stitches down their arms and sides and with a handgun in the backs of each of their belts, they slowly enter and stand staring at Hans, who's a little disconcerted by their strange presence.

What's all this? Bloody men! Or what is that, jam? That'd be sticky!

Various guests look around, but none seem to see what Hans is seeing.

6

Oh, other people can't see the blood-covered men . . . What blood-covered men?! Exactly! All part of a new story I am making up but which I will save for another day. 'The Blood-covered Men who Came to Tea'. See, I have so many stories they just keep popping out all over the place, don't they? Like an octopus in a straitjacket! Why a straitjacket popped into my mind at this moment, I do not know. Although my mum went mental! Yes, quite mental. She was a lowly, drunken washerwoman, and then she went mental. Not a great life-arc, but it's Denmark so, y'know? Edvard?!

Edvard 'Searching for her . . .'

Hans Searching for her?!

Hans notices one of the red men clear his throat and fold his arms.

Edvard The story . . .

Hans Ah yes! 'Searching for her . . . as if they knew she had thrown herself into the waves!' But then, guess what, 'Up she floated, with the other children of the air, to a rosy cloud that floated through the . . . aether . . .? Eva? Either? Ether . . .? 'And after three hundred years,' the sprite-lady says, 'thus shall *we* float into the Kingdom of Heaven. And we may even get there sooner, for every day we meet a good child . . .' Listen to this, you lot . . . 'Every day we meet a good child who is the joy of his parents and deserves their love, our time of probation is shortened. But whenever we see a naughty or a wicked child . . .'

He points at a fat kid.

'We shed tears of sorrow, and for every tear shed, a day is added to our time of trial.' A bit downbeat at the end, but 'The Little Mermaid' everybody, by me, Hans Christian Andersen!

A thunderous ovation, flowers thrown etc., as Hans comes down from the dais and shakes hands with all and sundry, keeping an eye on the bloody men, who are not applauding. In fact they gesture to the Press Man, who goes over to them, which strikes Hans as doubly strange, as he receives the approbation of Edvard and his daughter.

Edvard Oh my dear Hans! Oh it's your best, Hans! I think it's your best!

Hans Edvard Collin, you are just so gorgeous! Aren't you?! Look at you! Gorgeous! As a *person*, I mean. Not *gorgeous*. You have great taste as a *person*. I'm not in love with you or anything!

Edvard It appears as if you shall never run out of stories, Hans. How is it even possible?

Hans Well, it's just makey-uppy, isn't it? It's just what I do, I makey-uppy things. Is this your sickly daughter? Hello!

Ingrid Yes, Ingrid. We've met before.

Hans Have we?

Ingrid About a hundred times, yes.

Hans Well, I meet a lot of people, don't I, I'm very famous. Sandwiches, Edvard? (*To her.*) You can come too, Ingmar . . .

Hans leads Edvard off, arm in arm, taking a final look back at the red men who whisper something to the Press Man while pointing at Hans, which startles the Press Man immensely, and he is the last to leave the stage. Disturbed.

Blackout.

SCENE THREE

Night in the puppet attic. The box is resting on a wide shelf that runs most of the way across the room, and inside 'Marjory', the pygmy lady, sits writing. A couple of pages slip out through the paper slot and gently glide to the floor, as Hans swaggers in, slightly drunk.

Hans *Thunderous* applause! He exited to *thunderous* applause! What was the applause like what he exited to? Fucking *thunderous*!

Marjory Did the children like it?

Hans Like it? They *loved* it, mate. Even the thick ones. And there were loads of them, it was all rich kids.

Marjory They loved it? They loved 'The Little Black Mermaid'?

Hans Um . . . *everybody* loved it, reallly. Yeah. Although, y'know, I had to make a couple of changes. Minor changes.

Marjory Changes?

Hans Just to the title . . . and some bits about, y'know, the lead character.

Worried, Marjory comes to the front of the glass.

There's no such thing as black mermaids! Everybody knows that!

Marjory But . . .

Hans But what?!

Marjory There's no such thing as mermaids!

Hans Splitting hairs! At least I kept your stupid downbeat ending. I thought she should've married the prince! Not floated about in the aether/either for three

9

hundred years. Next story, *upbeat*. We've had enough death in the snow. Kids like a *bit* of dark, but seriously, send 'em to beddy-byes smiling. Like in real life. Unless they're chimney sweeps. I mean, I've had loads of sad stints in my life, I was a mental washerwoman's son, but now look at me. *Lauded*. *Worshipped*. The best writer about, and yet it all comes so easy to me.

Marjory quietly starts to cry, crumpling down.

Alright, to *us*. To *us*. Oh we're not having crying again this year, are we?

Marjory You *can't*!

Hans I can and I have, haven't I? Forever. 'The Little Mermaid'. No colour specified. Which means she's white, so suck it up. (*Pause.*) Come on, Marjory. I did get you a sausage!

He offers her the sausage through the hole. She takes it.

Marjory Can't you call me by my African name just once?

Hans No, I can't. It's too hard to remember. Too many 'M's and too many 'B's. 'Mbubba bububbaba'. *No*. '*Marjory*'. I *like* 'Marjory'. It's kind of like an ugly English princess! 'Is there any other kind?' cry the chorus!

Marjory Then can't I at least come out of the box for an evening? I'm sure our stories would be much less downbeat if I had a view of the birds and the trees and the rooftops to hold on to.

Hans They're pretty good already with just the things you can see from a two-inch sausage-hole.

She looks crestfallen again.

But . . . I suppose . . .

She brightens.

You remember what the payment was the *last time* I let you out, of course . . .

Marjory No! You're not having another foot! I've only got one left!

Hans Ah, I don't feel like sawing tonight anyway. Too splashy. And I'm a bit tired from all the plaudits. Fucking *thunderous* it was!

Marjory thinks for a moment.

Marjory 'And each night he would let her out of the box, because he wasn't such a bad man. Yet each morning, when he put her back inside, he would have made the box *one inch smaller*, because I was lying before when I said he wasn't such a bad man, he was terrible, actually.'

Hans thinks about it.

Hans Ooh, I like that, making the box smaller, cos it plays into my other thing I am brilliant at . . .

He waves at the terribly made ladder under the window . . .

Carpentry!

He undoes the heavy screws holding the glass in place.

Three inches smaller . . .

Marjory *One* inch smaller, for fuck's sake!

Hans Alright! Grumpy.

He slides the glass side down, allowing her to step out, stretch and idle along the shelf on her poorly made crutch, checking out the puppets she passes . . .

Marjory (*singing*)
'One day my Prince shall come.
One day my Prince shall come.
He'll call me by my name.
He'll free me from the ring
Of Hell I'm dwelling in.
He'll bring a gun.
He'll bring a gun.

'And all the world will rue
And all the world will rue
What Europe did to you.
Ten million skulls will bring
A dreadful reckoning
From Hell to you
From Hell to you.'

Hans takes the saw and the slide-rule that are attached to the top of the box and starts sawing into it.

Hans (*gleefully*) You'll get crushed to bits if we do this too many times!

Marjory Yes. Did the children really like 'The Little Mermaid'?

Hans Fucking *loved* it, mate! My agent said it was 'one for the ages'!

Marjory That's agents though, ain't it? Bullshitters.

Hans Oy! Ah, look at the little crutch I made ya. See, you can't say I'm all bad! You're like a tinier Tiny Tim! But African and not as funny.

Marjory I liked Tiny Tim. I like doomed cripples in stories who die. I was sorry he came back alive at the end. Even if it *was* Christmas.

Hans That, right there, is everything that's wrong with your attitude. Our new mantra is 'Upbeat, *yes* . . .'

Marjory 'Upbeat, *yes* . . .'

Hans 'Doomed cripples who die at Christmas . . .

Marjory (*smiling, same time as 'No'*) '*Maybe* . . .'

Hans No, not 'maybe'. *No.* Which reminds me! Charles Darwin has just invited me to come and stay at his house in London . . .!

Marjory Charles *Dickens* . . .

Hans Charles *Dickens* has just invited me to come and stay at his house in London because he thinks I'm totally fantastic! I think he's quite good too, although I haven't read any of his things, they're all too long, but he was very nice to me ten years ago when I met him at a party for what looked like a lot of high-class prostitutes in Dorset. We've been corresponding ever since. Well, *I* have. He's too busy. But it seems like we've got so much in common.

Marjory Like what?

Hans I dunno. *He's* a writer, *we're* a writer. *He* likes the poor, *you* like the poor. All our charity works for Africa. I think his mum might've died mental too but I'm not sure, I'll have to ask him.

Marjory Just remember to leave *food* this time.

Hans Yeah, yeah. Talking of remembering things . . .!

He takes out a bunch of letters from his jacket.

I just remembered my fan mail! Yay!

He starts going through the envelopes.

What've we got . . . poor kids, poor kids, poor kids . . .

He tosses all those away behind him.

Ooh, what's this! A letter from the King of the Spaniards! My gosh! A proper *seal* too, look. Classy!

Marjory comes and sits beside him, playing with a spider puppet.

Marjory *I'd* like to get a letter from a proper seal.

He gives her a look.

Hans As I say, a letter from the King of the Spaniards! 'Dear Hans Christian Andersen . . .' Ooh, a little formal, but that's okay. 'Your one about the duckies, it was great . . .' He must mean 'The Ugly Duckling'. 'Duckies!' Sweet King! 'And we at the Palace are *usually* quite delighted at all your new stories . . .' There's a 'usually' in there I'm not keen on. 'However . . .' Ooh, a 'however' too, even worse. 'However, "The Emperor's New Clothes" has us quite perplexed.' 'Perplexed' is alright, just means *he's* thick. 'I don't know nothing about *emperors*, but, as a *king*, which is *like* an emperor, no way would I go around with my cock and my balls out for all the world to see. No way would I do that, even if it *was* fashionable. And surely people would notice my cock and my balls out, and mention it, not just some little girl? And is that right anyway, to be showing my cock and my balls to some little girl in a children's story? She must be only about seven years old, this girl. Surely there are some moral implications to my cock and my balls right there in her face? In this little girl's face? Or am I reading it wrong? Yours sincerely, the King of the Spaniards.' (*Pause.*) Well, I think he's missed the satirical aspects entirely.

Marjory He's missed the satirical aspects, yes . . .

Hans He's reading it too literal, isn't he? A positive letter though, overall! And from a King, no less! Brilliant to get a letter from a King, isn't it? Even if it is just Spain.

Marjory A day will come when there are no kings and there are no queens. People still won't love each other quite as they ought to, it won't solve everything, but at least there'll be a few less cunts in the world we're paying through the teeth for.

Hans Do you want to go back in the box?

Marjory King Leopold the Second of Belgium, for instance.

Hans The Belgian Congo King? Your *bête noir*?

Marjory Now there was a cunt.

Hans You're just jealous cos he's rich and you're poor, and he killed nine million people in Africa and you didn't.

She gets up and wanders again.

Marjory *Ten* million people in Africa.

Hans Nine, ten, it's hard to remember when the numbers get that big, isn't it? Let's just say 'lots'. But I bet there'll still be statues up to him in Belgium in a hundred years' time. There won't be none to you. People *like* kings. African dwarfs they can take or leave.

Marjory We had kings and queens in Africa.

Hans Did ya?

Marjory Yeah. They were cunts there too.

Hans Let's have no more of the C-word, please. Ooh, a letter all the way from Oireland. From little Maureen, aged eight. Sure, we'll give her a go! Appalling handwriting, but I suppose it *is* Ireland.

Marjory wanders up the ladder to the window with some pigeon puppets.

Perhaps Maureen was using a little potato, dipped in ink?! Aren't I mean?!

Marjory If she's writing from Ireland in the 1850s, and if she could find a potato, I doubt if she'd be dipping it in ink.

Hans What's that, current affairs? Way over my head.

Marjory They don't have any potatoes there now.

Hans How sad! When it's what they're famous for. 'Dear Hans . . .' A little informal! 'I did read . . .' I'll do it in my Irish voice . . . 'I did read your wonderful story, "The Little Match Girl", and it brought a tear to me eye, so it did. For didn't it remind me of me own harsh life . . .' Here we go, begging letter . . . 'Me own harsh life, orphaned and destitute at the age of eight . . .' Hang on, she's eight and she's using big words like 'destitute'? I don't think so, Maureen! Her mum probably wrote this . . . Blah blah blah 'Had to bury the youngest in a Connemara peat bog . . .' blah blah blah . . . 'Yet all I could ever wish for . . .' Here we go . . . 'Would be a photograph from Hans Christian Andersen . . .' Oh . . . 'The man who taught children the world o'er how to dream again. Yours sincerely, Maureen . . . Currflurrrgghh . . .' I'm not even going to *try* to pronounce that! It's worse than yours! (*Pause.*) Hmm. Turned out not so irritating by the end. Poor Maureen. But come on, a signed photo all the way from Denmark? I'm not made of stamps, Maureen!

He tosses the letter away.

Marjory They'll be alright. They'll be free soon.

Hans Don't get any funny window ideas, by the way. That reinforced glass cost shitloads.

Marjory If I'd wanted to escape, I'd've escaped years ago.

Hans Says you.

Marjory I can't leave until it arrives, anyway.

Hans Until what arrives?

Marjory My future.

Hans Gobbledygook was the first signpost on my mum's flightpath to the nuthouse, so you just watch yourself.

Marjory What did you do with my foot, by the way?

Hans Your little foot? I sold it to gypsies for a haunted concertina. Well, they *said* it was haunted. I've been too scared to play it!

He gestures to the concertina on the wall and makes a scared face.

Marjory Yes, I hate haunted musical instruments. The bagpipes especially.

Hans And my final fan mail for this week comes from . . . Ooh, 'Anonymous'. Jerk! 'Dear Andersen . . .' Well, that's a bit, I don't know *what* that is . . .

Marjory Abrupt?

Hans Abrupt, yes. 'Dear Andersen, how come all your stories seem like they could have been written by a black midget imprisoned in a three-foot box?'

They exchange a look, then Marjory comes back down the ladder to sit beside him again. As she listens she plays with a kitten puppet, along with the pigeon ones.

' "Thumbelina", for instance. A tiny woman, befriended by bugs, and rescued by a bird. Or "The Shadow". A writer, after a strange trip to Africa, becomes haunted by his own shadow, a shadow that turns out to be smarter than the writer, takes over his entire life, and then executes him. All things that, most likely, only a very clever pygmy woman . . . chained up in a three-foot box . . . with one glass side and a two-inch sausage hole . . .

might dream up. You heard me, Andersen. A pygmy woman chained up in a three-foot box.'

They look at each other, then he gestures to the pigeon and kitten puppets she's playing with.

Well, that's put the cat amongst the pigeons! (*Pause.*) He was wrong about the *chains*, at least. Him or her.

Marjory Or *them*.

Hans Or *them*.

Marjory (*pause*) There wasn't anyone unusual at the reading today, was there?

Hans Unusual? No. No one that springs to mi— Unusual how?

Marjory A pair of brothers, covered in blood, perhaps?

Hans Not that I noticed. (*Pause.*) But there were a lot of people there, y'know? I'm very famous. (*Pause.*) What else might they have looked like? These non-existent brothers.

Marjory Carrying guns, perhaps? Or Belgian-sounding?

Hans Belgian-sounding? Well, they didn't say anything.

Marjory Who didn't say anything?

Hans (*pause*) Quite.

They both stare out front.

Blackout.

SCENE FOUR

The bloody Belgians, Dirk and Barry, in a spotlight or somesuch.

Barry Bicycles!

Dirk You won't believe us!

Barry It was bicycles, wasn't it?

Dirk It seems so innocuous now, but yes!

Barry Everybody loves bicycles, don't they? But because of bicycles . . .

Dirk We had to kill ten million people in the Congo.

Barry Incongruous! That was what *I* said!

Dirk It was the rubber, you see?

Barry For the tyres.

Dirk They had rubber down there . . .

Barry And we didn't have any rubber in Belgium, so . . .

Dirk Market forces, isn't it?

Barry King Leopold the Second . . .

Dirk The one with the beard . . .

Barry He liked bicycles and he felt like having a colony in Africa, so . . .

Dirk Everybody else had a colony in Africa! Why shouldn't Belgium have a colony in Africa?!

Barry Hard to argue with that logic.

Dirk So we'd go into the villages where the rubber quotas weren't met . . .

Barry And you'd lop a few hands off, it made sense at the start . . .

Dirk You'd've thought it would've concentrated their minds!

Barry *I'd* collect more rubber if I knew *my* hand or hands, or my *children's* hand or hands, were going to be chopped off, wouldn't you?

Dirk In retrospect we can see it's harder to work the less hands you have.

Barry Also, you would usually die.

Dirk So it just became a vicious circle, didn't it?

Barry Yes, like a massive spinning bicycle wheel that never . . . stopped . . . killing . . . blacks.

Dirk There'd be buckets of fucking hands all over the fucking place.

Barry There'd be villages massacred, willy-nilly.

Dirk That was *Lieutenant* Willy Nilly from Antwerp. He was a bad 'un!

Barry But not all of us liked killing men, women and children . . .

Dirk It would leave a terrible taste . . .

Barry That's why we'd go into the pygmy villages and kill *them* instead.

Dirk Yes, it felt more palatable when everybody was the same height.

Barry And you wouldn't have to run about so quick.

Dirk In retrospect, again, possibly unsound reasoning.

  Pause.

Barry Joseph Conrad's *Heart of Darkness* was inspired by the Belgian Congo . . .

Dirk So you can't say the Congo didn't get anything out of it.

Barry That'd be the positives of your import/export trade.

Dirk Anyway, that's where we first met Marjory.

Barry Or Mbute, or whatever her name is . . .

Dirk In one of the pygmy villages.

Barry That was where she killed us.

Pause.

Dirk The cow!

Barry Of course, none of this has happened yet . . .

Dirk None of this will happen for twenty-seven years . . .

Barry That's why we've come back.

Dirk To nip it in the bud.

Barry She thinks she can stop it ever happening.

Dirk That's why *she* came back.

Barry She can't stop it ever happening! It happened!

Dirk She's clever, but she's not *that* fucking clever!

Barry She can't stop it ever happening, can she?

They look at each other a moment. Worried. Then look back out front.

Dirk Ten million people!

Barry That's a lot of fucking people!

Dirk If you think about it.

Blackout.

In the blackout, sounds of chopping and sawing, then lights up on Hans making the box an inch (or so) smaller, as Marjory, or the Narrator, recites her new story, possibly through a megaphone.

Marjory / Narrator He grew up in a church basement in Tennessee and he didn't get along well with his seven older brothers. They would beat and bully him about how much he loved the gentle words of Jesus that'd filter down through the church's floorboards and fill his rebel heart with peace and love and all that type of stuff. But then this one day, boy, he went and did it! He set free all the little bugs and tiny creatures his brothers had caught in their traps down there, like he thought Jesus would've if *He* lived down there and cared about bugs. But when his brothers found out, oh boy was that the final straw! So they caught him and they held him up by his eight little arms and they nailed them to a block of wood, and they left him to die down there. And he died down there . . .

Marjory takes out the spider marionette from behind her back, makes it flutter gently . . .

But his soul didn't die. His soul rose up; it rose up past the cobwebs, past the floorboards, past the priests and the congregation. It rose all the way up to Heaven, in fact. But the man at the gates said they didn't let spiders into Heaven, cos 'It'd just scare the little kids.' And he floated back down. And he doesn't know where he is now. He doesn't know where he is. He just knows it's very very very very dark.

Hans has finished crafting the smaller box. Marjory turns to face it, shoulders slumped.

Hans What was it I said before?

Marjory Upbeat?

Hans We're getting somewhere now.

He gestures with a lazy thumb for her to get in the box. She indicates the spider puppet.

Marjory Can I keep this?

Hans I want to say no . . . so I'm going to say no.

He takes it from her. She gets into the box.

Puppet strings and pygmy necks . . . do . . . not . . . mix. As they say in Sweden.

He slides the glass up and locks her in. He gives the box a little push and it gently swings from side to side, as he moves away.

How's your new little box? Cosy?

Marjory Feels like more than a fucking inch.

Hans It could be two, I'm not very good at measuring, but maybe it'll concentrate your mind on something a little more *upbeat*. Brand new mantra, Marjory – Upbeat, yes. Crucified spiders who can't get into Heaven, less so.

He turns the box so the glass side faces away from us, the circular hole to us. He takes out a long string of sausages from inside his jacket.

Oh, I forgot to mention, I'm, uh, going on a little trip to England. For a couple of weeks.

Marjory's eye appears at the hole.

Marjory For a couple of weeks?

Hans This Charles Darwin invite . . .

Marjory Dickens . . .

Hans This Charles Dickens invite. But I've got you fourteen sausages, one for every evening I'm away. Fingers crossed the boat don't sink or we'll both be fucked! Don't stuff yourself!

He hands her one end of the string of sausages, letting the rest hang limp across the floor. He exits, and we hear the sound of him locking the attic door and his footsteps away downstairs. We see Marjory's eye and hand holding on to the sausages through the hole for a moment. Then she tosses them away and on to the floor, out of reach. Her eye backs away from the hole and disappears in the darkness there.

Blackout.

SCENE SIX

The box is still on the platform, back to us, the sausages still on the floor where Marjory tossed them. All the puppets on the back walls are more or less in their same positions, though the scarecrow puppet may have slumped a little, unbeknownst to us. The attic door is tried, then the lock is picked, and the Press Man from Scene Two quietly enters. He strikes a match and looks over the puppets, the sausages, then sees the box, and slowly walks over to it. He peers in through the circular hole, and as he does so the scarecrow puppet creepily stirs and lifts its head to reveal Hans, who watches all, as the grandfather clock beside him strikes seven. The Press Man, still not having seen Hans, slowly rotates the box so that the glass side faces him and us, as Hans quietly takes down a puppet of a woodsman, and takes the real-life axe from its hands. The Press Man strikes another match to see more clearly, and taps on the glass. There's a crumpled blanket but not much more inside it. Hans coughs, to finally get his attention.

Press Man Oh. Shit. Hello again.

Hans scratches his nose with the axe.

What's the axe for?

Hans For axing things. Don't axe stupid questions.

Marjory's disembodied snort is heard from somewhere, maybe even amplified, but the Press Man can't work out from where, though nothing has stirred in the box.

Press Man For axing what?

Hans For axing *whom*.

Marjory For axing *who*.

Hans Oh, I thought it was 'whom' when we don't know whom we're axing.

Marjory We *do* know whom we're axing.

Hans *We* do. *He* doesn't.

Press Man Well I do *now*!

Hans Oh, he does now.

Press Man (*whispered, but amplified*) Tell him you're only kidding about killing him.

Hans I'm only kidding about killing you.

Press Man (*whispered*) To reassure him.

Hans To reassure you.

Marjory No, don't *tell him* you're reassuring him!

Hans No, I don't *tell you* I'm reassuring you!

Press Man You come closer I'll smash this glass, and that's two of us you'll have to take on.

Hans There's no one in there, fuckhead.

He indicates a 'puppet' hanging on a crucifix on the back wall. It raises its head to reveal it's Marjory hanging there. She gives a little wave.

I saw you coming up the stairs, fool! You call that creeping? Fucking elephant feet!

Press Man You *do* keep a pygmy in your attic.

Hans Who says I do? Alright, yes I do. But saying that isn't going to make it *less* likely that you're going to get killed, is it? It's going to make it *more* likely.

Marjory But yes, *who says* he keeps a pygmy in his attic?

He turns to her.

Press Man Oh . . . well, a good journalist never reveals his sources, does he . . .?

Hans thwacks the Press Man across the head with the axe. He slumps down, bleeding . . .

Hans A good journalist?! You're a burgular!

Marjory *Burglar.*

Hans *Burglar.* An elephant-footed burgular!

Marjory Who told you?!

Press Man The red men . . . !

Marjory gets down off the cross. She and Hans exchange a look.

Marjory How did they know?

Press Man I don't know! I swear I don't!

Marjory Were they Belgian?

Press Man Yes, I think so. They had dark hair and a massive inferiority complex.

Hans That's Belgians alright! And was it blood or was it jam?

Marjory Hans, for Christ's sake! Of course it was blood. It was thirty-year-old Congo blood.

Hans That doesn't sound very hygienic.

Press Man I'm bleeding . . .

Hans Course you're bleeding. What did you think it was, axe-grease?

Press Man What's the greatest writer in all of Denmark doing with a pygmy in his attic?

Marjory What's the greatest writer in all of Denmark doing with a Hans Christian Andersen living downstairs from her?

Press Man (*pause*) She writes your stories?

Hans No. Sort of. We co-write them. I just don't do any of the writing. I change the bits I don't like and then erase all the rest from history. I'm more like a German theatre director. Or, y'know, a German generally.

Press Man This is something of a scoop.

Hans The scoop of a dead man, unfortunately.

Marjory Ooh, I quite like that, 'The scoop of a dead man.'

Hans Did you like that? See, I'm not a complete knobhead, am I?

Press Man Please. I've got my blind mother to look after.

Hans (*yawning*) Do ya?

Press Man I'm all she's got.

Hans Where's that whiny violin coming from? Oh yes, your mouth!

Press Man She's not just blind, she's deaf and dumb too, the poor thing.

Hans She's blind, deaf and dumb? She'll hardly notice you're gone!

Press Man (*to Marjory*) Please, Miss . . . They told me about your *sister*, too, the Belgians.

Marjory What about my sister?

Hans Now now . . . !

Marjory My sister's dead.

Press Man No, no. She's in a box in Charles Dickens's house in London.

Hans grabs the Press Man and, with his back to us, slits his throat with the axe, blood splattering across the glass of the box. Hans lets his dead body slump to the floor, then stands there, picking his fingers guiltily.

Hans 'Charles Dickens's house in London'! Like someone that famous would have a . . . pygmy in a . . .

Marjory looks at him, dumbfounded. Hans checks his watch.

Anyway, like I said, I'm off to Charles Dickens's house in London. There's a lot we have to catch up on. You'd better get back in the box.

Marjory She's alive?

Hans I don't know what you're talking about.

Marjory She's alive?

Hans Box, please.

She gets back in the box. He locks it up.

And *do* you want your sausages or *don't* you want your sausages, cos I'm aware of that sausage hissy-fit from earlier?

Marjory Is she alive, Hans?

Hans Maybe. I did say we had a lot in common, didn't I? (*Pause.*) Do you want me to pass on a message?

She goes to speak.

No, I'm only mucking about. I'm not some kinda 'message-passer-onner' am I? I'll see you in a couple of weeks, Marjory. Fingers crossed!

He puts the string of sausages back in through the hole, and exits . . . then comes back in again and turns down the gas lamp by the door.

I'll turn the lights off, eh? Save a bit of gas, I'm not made of money.

The lights dim and he exits again, his footsteps echoing away downstairs, leaving Marjory moonlit.

Marjory She's alive!

Smiling, she lays down under her blanket, and starts eating a sausage. The Narrator coughs, then speaks.

Narrator I'm jumping way ahead of myself here . . . but time travel allows that, so, y'know . . . (*Pause.*) Eighteen years after the events of Part One, and ten years before the horrors in the Congo were to begin, the esteemed Danish short-story writer, Hans Christian Andersen, died in Copenhagen of natural causes, following complications that arose from a fall out of bed . . . I swear to God, look it up! (*Pause.*) Amongst his belongings when he died, which mainly consisted of unsent love letters to both men and women and an attic-full of puppets made of materials that hadn't been invented yet, a very small mahogany box was found. Inside the box lay a tiny skeleton. It, too, was strung like a marionette: seventeen strings drilled into its arm bones and sixteen strings drilled into its skull . . .

As we hear this description we see, suspended inside the glass of the box above Marjory, the pygmy skeleton as described, neck and arms hanging from puppet strings . . .

It only had one foot left on it and it only had one hand left on it, and I'm not sure *how* Hans Christian Andersen is going to come out of this story *cleanly*, but remember children, it is only a story, and right now the story is only half over. So kick your shoes off and settle in, for the far more cheery and more or less upbeat Part Two.

As the narration ends, the skeleton slowly raises its skull, its vacant black eye sockets staring straight out at us.

Blackout.

End of Part One.

Part Two

SCENE SEVEN

*A pygmy woman enters, playing the haunted concertina –
a creepy, vaguely Chinese melody – and as she turns to
us we see that she is blind, her eyes gouged out some
time ago, just as, inside the box, Marjory awakes,
startled, and it's clear for the first time that the other
pygmy isn't her . . .*

Marjory Ogechi?! Ogechi?! Sister, is it you?! Look at me,
Ogechi!

*Ogechi laughs a creepy high-pitched laugh, and
continues playing.*

Put down the haunted concertina, Ogechi. It's making
you sound creepy.

Ogechi stops playing.

Can you reach the locks on the box, Ogechi?

Ogechi *Chinese!*

Marjory What?

Ogechi *Chinese!* You should have made the mermaid
Chinese. Those are the scariest mermaids. *Chinese!*

Marjory I didn't want her to be scary. I wanted the
children to like her.

Ogechi Chinese ghosts are the scariest ghosts, and
Chinese mermaids are the scariest mermaids. I don't
know why. Chinese children are cute, but *dead* Chinese
children are fucking *terrifying*. Even the Chinese agree!

Marjory Oh Jesus, it's a dream sequence.

Ogechi I'll tell you a creepy Chinese story now. Keep your hopes up!

Marjory This will not be good.

Ogechi gently plays the concertina as background to her creepy story.

Ogechi A Chinese Siamese twin had his throat slit . . .

Marjory Knew it!

Ogechi But his conjoined twin brother knew nothing about it, for his conjoined twin brother was deaf and blind, you see . . .

Marjory It gets worse!

Ogechi The slit-throat brother died there and then in their Shanghai hovel but his brother didn't die there and then. He just couldn't work out why they weren't walking any more, or talking any more, or eating any more. He thought he'd done something wrong, but he couldn't work out what. How cruel the world can be to the sensitive. To kill one half of a Siamese twin, and leave the other half not knowing, in a room with no food and no heat, and in the wintertime too. That's a box it'd be hard to write yourself out of, and he didn't, the poor sap. He died five days later, and some said he starved, and some say it was the cold that got him. Some even said he died of a broken heart, but no. He died of his brother's rigor-mortis. The first person ever to die of someone else's rigor-mortis. It crept up his sides, it crept up his insides, it crept up his lungs and his arms and it crept up his jawbone. The final thing it crept up was his left eyeball, just as a last tear fell from it, on to a cheek that had already gone cold. So, thinking it over, if he was still crying at that stage, maybe it *was* the sadness that got him. Maybe it *was* the sadness. (*Pause.*) That story is over now.

Marjory How was *that* supposed to keep my hopes up?

Ogechi finishes the tune and hangs the concertina on the wall where it was previously.

Ogechi I'd best get back to London. They'll be missing me.

She laughs her creepy laugh again.

Marjory (*tearfully*) Ogechi . . .!

Ogechi Don't forget where I've hung the haunted concertina. It might come in handy someday. If you ever wanna play some creepy Chinese shit.

She goes to the door.

Marjory Are you dead, Ogechi? Is that what this is?

Ogechi looks down at the ground sadly.

This isn't a dream sequence, is it? It's a *ghost* sequence.

Ogechi sadly exits, pulling the door closed behind her.

Goodbye, Ogechi.

Blackout.

SCENE EIGHT

A big dinner table at Charles Dickens's house. Dickens, his wife Catherine, and three of their children, Kate, Walter and Charles Jnr towards one side of the table, Hans to the other. Dickens is already apoplectic . . .

Hans Scusi, no, no, but in quite seriously, Mr Darwin . . .

Dickens Dickens! Mr Dickens! Mr Charles fucking Dickens! I've only been telling you that for five fucking weeks!

Hans Dickens, I know! Over and over, don't I . . . ?!

Dickens How many more times?!

Hans I know, isn't it . . .?

Dickens *I'm* the Christmas Cripples! *He's* the Origin of the Fucking Species!

Hans Pero, again, my Dickie, you will have to speak far more slowwwly et preciiisely if you wish a poor gangly fellow from the Danish lands to follow what it is you are talking, see?

Dickens I'll be precise, I'll be precise. When are you going to fucking leave?! It's been five fucking weeks, mate! You said it'd be two when you first turned up, and I nearly choked at two! But five!

Hans No, it's . . . I love the sound of your talking but it's, oh, it's so going over my head, do you see?

Kate Daddy says he doesn't like you and he wishes you would leave.

Catherine Katie, dear, that's not what he said.

Walter *Fucking* leave, he said.

Catherine Walter . . .

Dickens It's not that I don't like him. He's just doing my fucking head in!

Hans All I am hearing is something about an orchard. Which is wonderful, for I love orchards. For that is where one will find . . . (*To Charles Jnr.*) Charles?

Charles Jnr (*moodily*) Apples.

Hans Bravo! And the Danish word for apples?

Charles Aeble.

Hans Aeble, wonderful! What a clever urch! Can I squeeze you?

Charles Jnr No.

Hans Perfect!

Dickens Five weeks of this shit! I mean . . . it's not like I don't have other things to do!

Catherine And who's the lucky lady *this* week, Charles?

Dickens Oh don't *you* fucking start. I've had enough shit from lanky to last me a lifetime. I don't need you in me fucking earhole an' all.

Catherine Come, children. As your father is being a cock, I believe it is time for your bedtimes.

Walter Cock!

Hans The bedtimes of the little children. Delightful. Soap!

Kate Is Daddy banging the broads again, Mummy?

Catherine 'Again' suggests there was a time when Daddy *wasn't* banging the broads, that he then *restarted* banging the broads, so your terminology, Kate, isn't quite on the button, is it, darling?

Walter 'Terminology', class!

Hans The talk of the little children, it is like music, the Handel water music, no?

Walter Arsehole.

Charles Jnr Cretin.

Kate Leave!! Leave!!

The children file out, their mother close behind.

Catherine Goodnight, Mister Andersen. I'm quite sure we'll see you again in the morning and the following morning, and every morning until I and the children are all quite dead, I daresay.

Hans Bon jeurney! Up the stairs. So true!

Catherine exits too, giving Dickens a dirty look on the way.

The nicest children I ever met and, boy, have I met a shitload of children. Some Swiss!

Dickens gets up and pours himself a scotch.

Dickens It's all just senseless nonsense, everything you say. Just senseless fucking nonsense.

Hans No, none for me, Charles.

Dickens I didn't ask.

Hans Yes. My mama was always a mad one for the booze. And then she became a mad one for the everything. I wonder if one precipped the other? Nothing to do with me, so I don't care. What happened *your* old mum, Chuck?

Dickens Yes, I get half a word every ten words and the rest is just nonsense.

Hans gets a little conspiritorial now, ushering Dickens over, placing his words a little more . . .

Hans I not been able to ask you so far, what with the skank, but . . . how ees the writeeng? (*Mimes.*) The writeeng?

Dickens The writing? Oh. So so, Hans. So so.

Hans So so? Malo? Gloomy face? No good?

Dickens Malo, indeed. 'The Mystery of Edwin Drood'. *Fucked.*

Hans Miserere Drooge fucked?

Dickens I'm sorry I've been short-tempered, Hans. I *have* been fucking around behind Catherine's back, but it's not just that.

Hans No? Yes? The sky, perhaps?

Dickens The sky?

Hans (*pointing upwards*) Mothers?

Dickens I'll just go on with what I was saying while ignoring you, Hans. It seems to work better that way.

Hans Certainly. Post-bacon!

Dickens I feel like I'm a spent force, Hans. I'm not sure if I'll write another word, to be honest with you.

Hans I will try clear to make my talky, while the wife fuck orff upstairs.

Dickens While the wife fuck orff upstairs, I'm with you, Hans. I don't know how long I'll be with you, but for now I'm with you.

Hans Where ees Charles Dickens . . . Not Darwin! Dickens!

Dickens Not Darwin, that's right. *Dickens*!

Hans Dickens. Where ees Charles Dickens . . . *Marjory*?

Dickens I don't follow. 'Where is Charles Dickens Marjory?' That makes as little sense as everything you've been saying for five weeks.

Hans Scusi. (*Slowly.*) You have . . .

Dickens 'I have . . .'

Hans A . . .

Dickens 'I have a . . .' Good.

Hans Very little . . .

Dickens 'Very little.' This is good. 'I have a very little . . .' Don't say cock!

Hans You have a . . .

Dickens 'I have a . . .' We've been through this bit, 'I have a . . . '

Hans Very little . . .

Dickens 'I have a very little . . .' We're getting somewhere, slowly . . .

Hans Pygmy . . .

Dickens 'Pygmy'?

Hans Lidy . . .

Dickens 'Pygmy lidy?'

Hans In . . .

Dickens 'In . . .'

Hans A . . .

Dickens 'A . . .'

Hans *Box*.

He mimes a box.

Dickens 'I . . . ' Let me repeat, just to make . . . 'I have a . . . *pygmy lady* . . .' Are you sure about that bit so far?

Hans Pygmy lidy!

Dickens Pygmy lidy! 'I have a pygmy lady . . .'

Hans Pygmy lidy . . .

Dickens 'Pygmy lidy . . . in a box.'

Hans Claro. It is clear now.

Dickens I have a pygmy lady in a box.

Hans Like-a me, Dickie.

Dickens The sentence itself is clear and concise, it's just that it makes absolutely no fucking sense whatsoever. 'I have a pygmy lady in a box.'

Hans *You* have a pygmy lidy . . . (*Mimes a pygmy lady.*) *I* have a pygmy lidy . . . (*Mimes another pygmy lady.*)

Dickens *Ohh . . . I see . . .*

Hans You see?! Claro?! Pygmy lidy?

Dickens It hasn't just been an issue of the language barrier these past weeks, has it? No, on top of that, Hans Christian Andersen has gone stark raving mental. Just like his mother did. Stark raving mental. I *see*!

Hans *My* mother mental! *Your* mother mental!

Dickens *My* mother wasn't mental . . .

Hans *Your* . . .

Dickens *Yours* was.

Hans *Your* pygmy lidy normal, *my* pygmy lidy normal. My pygmy writey very good. Your pygmy writey . . . ? Question merk! *You* say.

Dickens Hans . . . why won't you just go home?!

Hans And orso . . .

Dickens Here we go . . . 'And also . . .'?

Hans Did you, Dickie . . .?

Dickens 'Did I, Dickie . . . ?'

Hans Sen . . .

Dickens Sen? Send? 'Did I send . . . ?'

Hans Me . . .

Dickens 'Did I send you . . . ?'

Hans The . . .

Dickens 'The . . . ?'

Hans Red men.

Dickens 'The red men'? 'Did I send you the red men?' People don't send people red men, Hans! And I know Denmark is a whole different culture, but people don't send people red men in Denmark either! I'm quite sure it's some kind of frontal lobe dysfunction, Hans. Maybe there's something that can be done with the right medication.

Hans No red men? L'hommes rouge, non?

Dickens There'll be people to look after you when you go back to Denmark, Hans. I bet your health system is *way* better than our health system.

Hans (*crestfallen*) No red men?

Dickens You've got to go home now, Hans.

Hans (*pointing*) Upstairs?

Dickens *No. Home.* It's been five weeks, mate.

Hans (*realising*) Five weeks?!

Dickens Five *fucking* weeks, I meant to say.

Hans Oh Marjory!

Dickens Oh Jesus!

   Blackout.

SCENE NINE

The puppet attic. Sounds of footsteps stomping up the stairs. Marjory awakes in the box – gaunt, weak, thin. She comes to the glass to listen as the door is tried, then kicked open, and the shadows of two men fill the room. She backs away to the rear of the box as the red men enter, slowly, singing a creepy Elizabethan roundelay. While singing, and slowly approaching the box, one picks up and plays with the spider puppet, the other takes out his gun, an old Webley . . .

Barry *and* **Dirk**
'Hey ho, nobody home.
Meat nor drink nor money have we none
Still I will be merry . . .

'Rose, rose, rose, rose,
Will I ever see thee wed?
I will marry at thy will, sire
At thy will.

'Ding dong, ding dong
Wedding bells on an April morn
Carve my name on a moss-covered stone
On a moss-covered stone.

'Ah poor bird!
Take thy flight!
Fly above the sorrows
Of this sad night.'

The song over, Dirk taps on the glass with his gun as Barry takes his gun out too. Marjory takes off the blanket she'd hidden herself in and comes to the front of the box.

Barry Hello again.

Marjory Hello again.

Dirk Fancy seeing you after all these years.

Marjory Yes. You haven't got any food, have you? I'm fucking starved.

They stare at her a moment, then Barry takes out a bag of chips with mayonnaise and gives it to her through the hole.

Barry I have, actually, I've got some chips with mayonnaise.

Marjory Thanks! (*She eats.*) Unusual.

Dirk We came here to execute her, Barry, not to feed her chips.

Barry We can be nice about it, can't we?

Dirk Wasted that whole creepy song now. Christ, it stinks in here.

Marjory indicates the dead, rotting Press Man with a chip.

Barry That nice newspaper man? Throat slit? Who did that?

Marjory Hans Christian Andersen.

Barry Fucking Hell! And everyone thinks he's so nice!

Marjory Tell me about it!

Dirk Where's your foot gone?

Marjory Andersen cut it off. Sold it to gypsies for a haunted concertina.

Barry What a fucking rotter!

Dirk I dunno. Maybe he did it so she wouldn't miss the old country, y'know? (*Smirks.*)

Barry Alright, Dirk. There's no need for that.

Dirk She stabbed my eye out with a bamboo stick!

Barry That's all in the past, isn't it? I mean, the *future*, isn't it?

Marjory hands the remainder of the chips back.

Marjory Not sure about the mayonnaise, to be honest.

Barry It'll catch on.

Marjory I dunno . . .

Barry *No.* It *will.*

Dirk Alright, enough about chips, let's just get this over with . . .

Dirk raises his gun to shoot her, but Barry pushes it back down . . .

Barry I am not shooting a pygmy in a box, Dirk. It'd be like shooting fish in a barrel, but with a pygmy. We'll let her out in the fresh air and stand her up against something. Y'know, like her husband and kids!

Barry starts undoing the glass panel as Dirk keeps his gun trained on Marjory.

Dirk Don't try anything clever.

Marjory It's hard for me not to.

Dirk Smartarse. Shorty smartarse.

Marjory Where's your other brother, by the way?

Barry We don't have another brother.

Marjory Yeah, you do. You were triplets the last time I killed you. Siamese triplets. You must've lost him in the time travel.

Barry is perturbed by this. He looks over the stitches that run up their arms and their sides.

Dirk Don't listen to her, Barry. She's just trying to mess with your head.

Barry It's fucking working, Dirk!

Dirk That's just what she does, isn't it? She makes things up.

Marjory He's right. Don't even think about it.

But Barry is still perturbed.

Dirk Have you always written, Marjory?

Marjory Yes. Since before I was a baby.

They look confused.

I've a thousand and two stories at this point. But I never had any paper, so they're all . . .

She taps her head.

Barry Wow. She's not just good at writing, she's also good at remembering!

Dirk Shame they'll all be lost then.

Marjory The story ain't over yet though, is it, boys?

She gives them a wink.

Barry She's very self-assured for a midget who's about to be executed.

Marjory It's the mayonnaise!

Dirk Shorty smartarse. Stand over there and shut up.

Marjory Are you going to do a countdown from ten or something, like in the duels?

Barry Well, it isn't a duel, is it?

Dirk We're Belgian, not French!

Barry We *were* going to just shoot you. There wasn't going to be any counting involved.

Marjory It would be more dramatic though, wouldn't it, a nice countdown? And I could play a little tune of farewell to my loved ones. It'll be a creepy tune, and slightly Chinese, but it'll be atmospheric!

Dirk I vote no.

Barry I vote it's the least we can do if you take the Congo into consideration.

Dirk I suppose we have come all this way.

Marjory Thank you.

She takes the concertina from the wall, and starts playing a haunted tune. They raise their guns as she does so, cock them, and aim at her . . .

Marjory Well, start then!

Barry *and* **Dirk** Oh! *We* start! I thought *you* started! Ten . . .!

The tune continues throughout.

Marjory All I ever wanted . . .

Both Men Nine!

Marjory Was to go asleep beside my husband and my babies . . .

Both Men Eight!

Marjory And let the stories inside my head . . .

Both Men Seven!

Marjory Rest in silence . . .

Both Men Six!

Marjory But then you killed my husband . . .

Both Men Five!

Marjory And then you killed my babies . . .

Both Men Four!

Marjory And my stories were all I had left to me . . .

Both Men Three!

Marjory And now you've killed them too.

Both Men Two!

Marjory And now you've killed them too.

Both Men One!

Marjory takes a deep breath shutting her eyes tight, the concertina is at its widest note, and just as the red men are about to shoot, we freeze this image in a Goya-like tableau . . .

Blackout.

SCENE TEN

The Dickens house. Hans's travel bag is on the table, and Dickens is hurriedly helping him put his large overcoat and hat on, as Catherine comes back in.

Hans I don't . . . Hah! I don't understand so quite so well . . .

Dickens That's alright! It's good not to understand things sometimes, isn't it? It leaves so much to explore in the future . . . (*To Catherine.*) I think I've got him to go . . .

Catherine You're shitting me!

Dickens Don't do or say anything that'll make him change his mind!

Hans There no red men?

Dickens There no red men, no . . . Buttons, that's it . . . He wasn't just Danish, Catherine, he was mental too!

Hans Orso and no pygmy? No pygmy in a box?

Dickens No, no pygmy in a box, Hans. No pygmies at all in London, a little known fact, eh, Catherine?

Catherine Yes, that's right. She died last year, the poor thing.

Dickens forces a smile, continuing to help with Hans's buttons.

Dickens No, that's . . . not helping, Catherine . . .

Hans Die, you say?

Dickens She didn't say anything *like* die!

Catherine Yes, she died on Christmas Day. The children were heartbroken until we gave them the train set.

Hans Your pygmy lidy die?

Dickens No, no, no, no, no . . .

Catherine Yes, didn't Charles tell you?

Dickens What did I just . . . Now he's never gonna fucking go!!

Hans Mister Darwin say . . .

Dickens Dickens!!

Hans Mister Darwin say you got no pygmy not nor never have have have have had no pygmy.

Catherine We *have* have had a pygmy. What are you talking about, Charles? Who else has been writing all this stuff while you've been fucking everything that moves?

Dickens (*sitting*) I don't need this. Do I need this? No, I don't need this!

Catherine So now you even lie about the women you *haven't* been sleeping with, let alone the ones you have, is that it?

Dickens looks away sheepishly.

Charles? I said, 'Now you even . . .' Oh Charles, you didn't . . .

Dickens Of course I didn't! What kind of a man do you take me for?

Catherine Oh God . . .

Knowing he's lying, Catherine sits at the table, drained.

Hans Little pygmy lidy die? And Mister Dickens lie? And Mister Andersen not mental?

Dickens Two of those three statements have an accuracy to them, I'll grant you.

He sadly gets up and, from a cupboard, takes out the skeleton of a pygmy woman that's been made into a marionette: seventeen strings attached to her arm bones and sixteen strings attached to her cranium. It has one hand and one foot missing.

The children sort of missed her, so we made her corpse into a marionette. But it's not the same. I can't finish 'Drood' now, and the house has felt so dreadfully empty since Christmastide. You don't really notice the sound of all that typing . . . until it's gone forever.

Hans Skeleton? From da cupboard?

Dickens Yes. There's probably a joke in there somewhere, but I don't know what it is!

Catherine Yes, you'd need someone to write it for you, wouldn't you, Charles?

Dickens Catherine, please!

Hans takes the skeleton.

Hans How your little Marjory go die?

Dickens How did my Marjory go die?

Hans Die, yes! Die, liar Dickie! Die!

Dickens Yes, I'm sorry I lied, Hans. I *am* sorry. It's just hard to admit, isn't it, that your whole life's work has been written by a tiny African woman you've imprisoned in a box. She didn't write it *all* though, in my defence . . .

Catherine Bollocks!

Dickens She just wrote the plots, and the characters . . . and the dialogue. And all the describing bits. I helped with the titles! 'Bleak House', that was mine. The one about the house . . . that was a bit bleak. (*Pause.*) 'Little Dorrit' . . . the one about . . . well, that's kind of self-explanatory. (*Pause.*) 'Medium-Sized Expectations' . . . No, she changed that one back, didn't she, so no.

Catherine I'm leaving you, Charles.

Dickens Catherine, stop it . . .

Catherine And I'm taking one of the children with me.

Dickens *One* of the children?

Catherine Yes, Katie. The others are annoying. Especially the slow one.

Dickens Which one's the slow one?

Catherine Exactly!

Hans How your little Marjory go die?

Dickens Well, it's a bit of a long story, but we know you've got the time.

Hans Yes . . .

He sits at the table, takes his hat off and undoes his buttons again. Dickens sighs.

Dickens Well, apparently, gypsies . . . Do you have that word in Danish, 'gypsies'?

Hans Gypos, yep.

Dickens Gypos, yes, gypsies . . . Apparently, gypsies – and I didn't know this at the time – but, apparently, gypsies are from the future come back in time to tell us that work is pointless and we should all get out in the fresh air a lot more, and I must say I concur with the concept, I just don't think they they go around explaining it in quite the right way. Anyway, somehow *my* Marjory . . . we actually called her 'Pamela', after Catherine's late aunt in Rochester . . . somehow Pamela got word to our local gypsy contingent to bring something back from the future for her, something she hoped she might one day find of use in the Congo. If she ever got up the money to go there, or, I suppose, *survived*. And so the gypsies came knocking at Christmas, as they do. I gave them her foot and one of her little hands, and they gave me what they called a haunted concertina, one of two they said they'd gotten ahold of. So I took it up to Pamela, didn't I, darling? And gave it to her, and for the first time in many many years her eyes lit up . . . her beautiful little eyes lit up . . .

Catherine gives him a sad look.

But it turns out the concertina wasn't haunted, they never are, it was just the best place to hide the machine gun they'd brought for her. And then, as you can imagine, all Hell broke loose . . .!

Blackout on the Dickens house and instant lights up on . . .

SCENE ELEVEN

The attic, as again the Belgians count down to –

Both Men One!

– whereupon Marjory lets rip with the machine gun hidden in her concertina, an insane deafening volley of gunfire that tears the Belgians to horrifying pieces, bloody squibs bursting out of them, Peckinpah-like in their awful death dance, arterial spray splattering the walls behind them, till they finally collapse to the blood-strewn floor in clumpen fucked-up heaps and, as they're lying there, Marjory gives them another burst of machine-gun fire for good measure. She steps back to observe her handiwork – Dirk dead, Barry almost . . .

Marjory Fucking Belgians!

Marjory takes the two guns from their hands or wherever they've fallen and places them on top of the concertina that she's put on the shelf . . .

Webleys, nice. Old-fashioned. Or is it *new*-fashioned, I get mixed up! But you can't have too many guns when you're off to save the Congo!

She looks around to figure out her next plan of action but is startled by Barry . . .

Barry Marjory?

Marjory Ooh, alive, hello . . .

She grabs a Webley again . . .

Barry Did we . . . did we really have another brother? A Siamese triplet brother that we lost while time-travelling?

Marjory Oh! No, no, I was just fucking around! You didn't believe me, did you?

Barry That was a bit mean, Marjory.

Marjory Me name's Mbute, bitch.

She kicks him in the head, and he dies. She puts the gun down on the concertina, does up her shirt and tucks it into her trousers, ready for action, grabs her wooden crutch . . .

Got me little crutch!

And limps over to something she's spotted on top of the box and picks up it up, happily – the spider marionette!

Not so dark now, is it, Spider? Not so dark now!

Just then, the shadow of Hans appears in the doorway and he enters. Marjory hurries towards the guns and the concertina but he's already beside them. He picks up the guns, and puts the concertina on. They stand looking at each other for quite some time.

Hans You will not believe the gall of that Charles fucking Dickens!

Marjory Oh no?

Hans He only tried to make me think that I'd gone bonkers!

Marjory Bonkers?! You?! Never!

Hans That's what *I* said! (*Pause.*) Ooh, I see the red men turned up.

Marjory Mm. I had to kill 'em and that.

Hans I can see! (*Pause.*) I expect they deserved it.

Marjory They will.

Hans Yeah, I get a bit confused with a lot of this time-travelling stuff!

Marjory How's my sister?

Hans (*pause*) Well . . .

Marjory (*hopefully*) Well?!

Hans No, not '*well*'! Christ no, not 'well'. '*Well*' . . . dot dot dot . . . '*she's*' . . . dot dot dot . . . '*dead*'. Dot.

Marjory Oh. I knew she was.

Hans Did you? Pygmies' intuition?

Marjory No. I just knew.

She sits down, sadly.

Hans I'm sorry, Marjory. Honest.

From a bag he pulls out Pamela's skeleton, strung up by puppet strings . . .

But I did bring her back for you.

Marjory What?! I knew she was dead! I didn't know she'd had a load of puppet strings stuck into her fucking head!

Hans Well *I* didn't do it! Don't shoot the messenger! It was that Charles Dickens fucker! That's what he's like!

She takes her sister in her arms.

You could tell he was a knob just from his beard. I am never going to that shitty little country again. The ugliest children in the world. We shouldn't have called it 'The Ugly Duckling', we should've called it 'The Ugly English Kid', be more believable. Except they wouldn't've grown out of it.

Marjory caresses the skeleton, lovingly, tearful . . .

Poor old . . . whatever her name was.

Marjory Ogechi.

Hans Ogechi?! Sounds Jap!

Marjory It means 'Time Spirit'.

Hans Oh yeah? And you go on about *me* being bad, at least I didn't take your foot *and* your hand off.

He lifts up Ogechi's missing part.

So in terms of who's the best looker-afterer, it's me, isn't it, really? *I* win.

Marjory No, she was already missing a hand and a foot. From the Congo.

Hans Oh really? That's weird. Well he's just a non-stop fucking liar, isn't he, that Dickens? I bet they'll still bury him in Poets' Corner. With all the other twats. (*Pause.*) He definitely slept with her, though. At least I never did that.

Marjory (*tearfully*) What?!

Hans Oh. Nothing!

Marjory What did you tell me *that* for?!

Hans Well . . . cos it happened, y'know. Cos it's true. Like the Congo. (*Pause.*) Which hasn't happened yet, it *will* happen, won't it . . . I told you I get confused.

Marjory It won't happen. I won't let it.

Hans Good for you. (*Pause.*) Dunno how you'll do that from a box in an attic in Copenhagen.

Pause.

I *do* win over Dickens then, don't I? At least I never did any of that funny business. I didn't even try!

Marjory That's just because you prefer men.

Hans I do not prefer men! Who says I prefer men?! Just because I do embroidery?

Marjory No. Just because you're in love with Edvard Collin.

Hans Am I? Who is? *I* am? Am I? (*Pause.*) He *is* nice though, isn't he?

Marjory I don't know. I've never met him. I've been in a box.

Hans Oh! I just got a letter from Edvard Collin on my way over, I completely forgot! In my haste to stop you executing half of Denmark. Perhaps he likes me too? 'Dear Hans . . .' Good start, bodes well . . . (*Reads.*) Oh. Nope. Just a loada stuff about . . . one of his daughters has died, apparently. How many is *that* now?! Glad I never met her! (*Reads.*) No, not a word about me. Selfish, some people. (*Folds the letter away.*) I still like him, though! Those eyes!

Marjory stands, and gently places the skeleton on to a shelf. They look at each other.

Well, I . . . I suppose it's about time you got back in the box, isn't it? (*Pause.*) In fact, how long have you been out of the box? I suppose we'll have to adjust it accordingly, if we're being fair.

Marjory Yes. Of course. But perhaps I could play you a little tune, Hans? Before the carpentry starts?

Hans You know I find haunted concertinas frightening.

Marjory You'll be fine after the first few notes.

Hans (*pause*) That's how I envisaged the story ending, you know? The box gets smaller and smaller, you get sadder and sadder, until, one day . . . pop! (*Pause.*) That's your head exploding, that pop.

Marjory That's a shit ending.

Hans Is it?

Marjory What's our mantra? Upbeat, *yes*. Sad pygmy lady getting squashed to bits until her head explodes . . . *no*!

Hans (*same time*) *Maybe* . . . I said *maybe* at the same time!

Pause. They stare at each other a long moment.

Marjory You know you'll have to kill me if you want me to get back in the box.

Hans (*pause*) I know.

Pause. He hands her the Webleys and hangs the concertina around her neck.

Safe travels.

They look at each other as she holds the guns on him a moment.

I haven't read up on it . . . because it's impossible to, it hasn't happened yet, but that doesn't sound like a barrel of laughs, the Congo in the late 1800s.

Marjory It'll be different this time.

Hans Ten million people. That's a lot of fucking people! It'll probably define the century.

Marjory It won't.

Hans Won't it?

Marjory Cos it won't happen. Coupla hundred dead Belgians, then everybody shuts the fuck up and goes the fuck home.

Hans Fingers crossed, eh? (*Pause.*) Talking of dead Belgians, who's going to clear up all these dead Belgians?

She looks at them.

Marjory Well it's not *my* fucking house, is it?

Hans Oy! Jerk!

Pause.

Marjory Well, I'll be off now then!

Hans Off to Africa then, yeah? Alright.

Marjory Yeah. No point putting it off, eh?

Hans Are you going to time-travel down there?

Marjory Nah, I'll probably just get the bus.

Hans Yes, I like the Danish Transport System, it's very clean and it's very efficient, although I'm pretty sure they don't go all the way to Africa. You'll at least have to change.

Marjory That's alright. I've got time.

They look at each other a moment . . . then shake hands.

Hans Yes. Very clean, Danish buses. (*Pause.*) Unlike Italian buses! My God! It's like they only let lepers use 'em! Which can't be right, can it, demographically, Italy, all just lepers? (*Pause.*) That'd be more Jerusalem.

Pause.

I'll miss you. (*Pause.*) Will you miss me?

Marjory No.

Pause. He nods. She turns to go. Finding the concertina a little clunky, she breaks it open to reveal the spanking new sub-machine gun inside it, tosses away the excess concertina –

Hans That's better. Less bulky on the bus.

– and, machine gun in hand, a Webley in each pocket, she prepares to go. She looks down at the dead red men, dips her hands in their blood and smears it all over her face and her clothes . . .

Ooh, they won't take kindly to that on the 176!

Marjory takes out a cigar, clenching it between her teeth.

Where'd you get that from?!

Marjory Cuba!

Hans You clever minx!

Marjory Fare thee well, Hans Christian Andersen.

Hans Oh. Fare thee well . . . Marjory . . . Christian Andersen.

She gives him a look of disdain.

Hans Fare thee well . . . Mbute Masakele.

Marjory It wasn't *that* fucking hard, was it?

Hans It was a *bit* hard, with the 'M's.

Marjory stands in the light of the doorway and lights the cigar . . .

Narrator And she lit a cigar. And she holstered her guns, and she strode out of the puppet attic, to go and save the Congo.

Time freezes strangely on stage.

Whether she succeeded or whether she failed, only time will tell us, really. It is a truth, though, a sad and sorry truth, that to this very day, all over Belgium – statues *still* stand to King Leopold the Second . . . always with a beard . . . often with a sword in his hands . . . never with blood on them . . . and as Marjory herself might say . . .

Marjory I ain't seen a statue to a pygmy in a long time, boys.

Narrator But, as Mbute might also say . . .

Marjory The story isn't over yet. Is it?

She winks at us . . . and exits to save the Congo. Hans watches her go, her long shadow very slowly disappearing out of the doorway. Hans stands, picks up Ogechi's skeleton, gently hangs it inside the mahogany box, closes up its glass side, and leaves it hanging there, creepily lit, as he sits on the shelf beside it. He surveys the room a moment: the skeleton, the rotting Press Man, the dead Belgians and their bloodstained walls, the doorway that Marjory departed through. Then he looks out front, nodding slightly.

Hans *Upbeat!* More or less. (*Pause.*) Be good if she did it though, wouldn't it?

He nods slightly, as the lights fade, to a creepy accordion tune, last lights lingering on Hans and the skeleton, then . . .

Blackout.

End.